AF483665

# Dedication

To my wonderful girls,
Hailey & Juniper—

This story began with your questions.
May you never stop asking "why."
Love you always & forever.

# Under One Sky

## A Child's Introduction to Six World Religions

Written & Illustrated By
Jessica Sutton

Hello! I'm Tin, Tin the Star,
I may be small, but see so far!
I twinkle softly through the night,
A fuzzy glow of gentle light.

From up above, I watch and see,
The many ways that folks can be.
I shine above the homes so small,
And notice kindness in them all.

From high above, a window glows,
A candle flickers soft and slow.
A quiet home beneath the night,
Is wrapped in calm and gentle light.

I pause to watch them sit and breathe,
As peaceful thoughts begin to weave.
They practice kindness, calm and true,
And share that warmth the whole day through.

Buddhism

Below, warm windows shining bright,
Soft colors glow into the night.
A gentle song begins to grow,
As voices rise both high and low.

I watch them stand and sing along,
Together sharing joyful song.
Their voices echo through the hall,
A joyful sound that welcomes all.

Christianity

Tiny points of light appear,
In peaceful homes both far and near.
They flicker softly in the night,
And warm each room with steady light.

Flowers set with so much care,
In a special place for all to share.
Families sitting calm and near,
Fill the night with warmth and cheer.

The sky turns gold, then pink, then blue,
I see a quiet, peaceful view.
In gentle rows they move below,
Beneath the sunset's fading glow.

I watch them bend and kneel down low,
In calm, slow waves, row after row.
So still and peaceful in the air,
A quiet moment that they share.

*Islam*

A row of candles shining bright,
One hand reaches out to share their light.
The braided loaf is placed with care,
As loved ones gather round to share.

I watch them sit together near,
Soft laughter drifts for me to hear.
They pass the bread and gently smile,
And stay and talk a little while.

*Judaism*

I see so many gathered round,
As busy steps and voices sound.
Some come and go, some stop to greet,
A place where helping hearts all meet.

Some carry plates from hand to hand,
And help each person where they stand.
They share their food and time and care,
And make sure all feel welcome there.

The sky turns soft with morning hue,
My time to shine is almost through.
The stars grow faint, the dark is gone,
I say goodbye and drift along.

I've seen so many ways to live,
So many ways to love and give.
Though all are different, near and far,
Each shines so bright, just like a star.

# For the "Why"

This story was created to help young readers explore the many ways people around the world find meaning, kindness, and connection.

Each page shows a simple moment from a different tradition. While these scenes cannot represent every belief or practice, they offer a gentle introduction to the beautiful diversity of faiths shared across our world.

Families may practice these traditions in many different ways, but at heart they often share values of compassion, community, reflection, and love.

## Buddhism ☸

Tin saw a family sitting quietly and breathing slowly in meditation. Many Buddhists practice meditation to calm their minds and find peace. Buddhism began in Asia and teaches kindness and awareness of how our actions affect others. Practicing calmness and compassion helps bring happiness to themselves and the world around them.

## Christianity ✝

Tin saw people gathered together singing in a place of worship. Many Christians meet to sing, pray, and listen to stories from the Bible. Christianity began in the Middle East and is now practiced around the world. Christians believe in loving others, helping those in need, and showing kindness each day.

## Hinduism ॐ

Tin saw a family sitting together at home, placing flowers and lighting small lamps called diyas (DEE-yahs). Hinduism began in India and includes many traditions and ways of worship. Some families have special places in their homes where they pray and give thanks. Many Hindus believe in caring for others, respecting life, and finding peace each day.

## Islam ☪

Tin saw people praying together at sunset, moving gently in rows, often on special prayer mats. Islam began in the Middle East and is practiced around the world. Muslims pray at certain times each day, at home or in a mosque. Many Muslims believe in caring for others and living with kindness and respect.

## Judaism ✡

Tin saw a family gathered at a table, lighting candles and sharing a braided loaf of bread called challah (HAH-luh). Judaism began in the Middle East and is one of the oldest religions in the world. Many Jewish families gather at home to celebrate special days and spend time together. Many Jewish people believe in caring for others, learning, and honoring their traditions.

## Sikhism ☬

Tin saw many people gathered together, serving and sharing food in a welcoming space. Sikhism began in South Asia and teaches the importance of helping others and treating everyone equally. In many Sikh places of worship, a community meal called langar (LUN-gur) is shared, where everyone is welcome to sit and eat together. Many Sikhs believe in kindness and serving others with respect and generosity.

Under One Sky: A Child's Introduction to Six World Religions

Written and illustrated by Jessica Sutton

First Edition

Printed in the United States of America

This book is a gentle introduction to several world religions and traditions. Practices and beliefs may vary across families and communities.

Questions or thoughts about this book?
You can reach the author at:
underoneseries@gmail.com

www.ingramcontent.com/pod-product-compliance
Lightning Source LLC
Chambersburg PA
CBHW040222110726

48005CB00019B/3116